# Dream of a Journey

# PARTHIAN

CYNGOR LLYFRAU CYMRU
BOOKS COUNCIL of WALES

MINISTRY OF CULTURE
CZECH REPUBLIC

This translation was made possible by a grant
from the Ministry of Culture of the Czech Republic

**Kateřina Rudčenková** is a poet, prose writer and playwright. Her poetry debut *Ludwig* (1999) and her second collection *Není nutné, abyste mě navštěvoval* (There Is No Need for You to Visit Me, 2001) established her as one of the most distinctive voices in contemporary Czech poetry. They were followed by *Popel a slast* (Ashes and Pleasure, 2004) and her fourth collection, *Chůze po dunách* (Walking on Dunes, 2013), which came almost a decade later and won her the prestigious Magnesia Litera Award. She has also published a collection of interlinked short stories, *Noci, noci* (Nights, Nights, 2004). Her plays have been translated and staged in various countries, including the United Kingdom as part of the Royal Court Theatre's international residency project.

**Alexandra Büchler** is director of the platform Literature Across Frontiers, as well as editor and translator of prose, poetry and texts on art and architecture between her native Czech, English and Greek, with close to thirty publications to her name. Among the authors she translated into Czech are J. M. Coetzee, Jean Rhys and David Malouf. She has edited and part-translated six anthologies of short fiction in translation, and between 2006 and 2016 was series editor of Arc Publications' bilingual anthologies *New Voices from Europe and Beyond*, sometimes referred to as the 'Six Poets' series, for which she prepared *Six Czech Poets*, 2007. Her English translation of the Czech modern classic *The House of a Thousand Floors* by Jan Weiss was published by CEU Press in 2016.

# Dream of a Journey

## Selected Poems

Kateřina Rudčenková

Edited and translated by Alexandra Büchler

PARTHIAN

Parthian, Cardigan SA43 1ED www.parthianbooks.com
First published in 2020
© Kateřina Rudčenková 2021
© This translation by Alexandra Büchler 2021
ISBN 978-1-913640-54-5
Editor: Alexandra Büchler
Cover image 'Ballet Mechnique' by Daniel Pitín
Cover design by Emily Courdelle
Typeset by Elaine Sharples
Printed and bound by 4edge Limited, UK
Published with the financial support of the Welsh Books Council and the Ministry of Culture of the Czech Republic
British Library Cataloguing in Publication Data
A cataloguing record for this book is available from the British Library.

# Contents

*from* **Walking on Dunes (2013)**

*Notes*
*Acknowledgements*

# Introduction

Kateřina Rudčenková is one of the most translated Czech women writers, whose early poems secured her a place in Arc Publications' *A Fine Line: New Poetry from Eastern and Central Europe* and *Six Czech Poets* already in the mid-2000s. More recently, her work appeared in *The World for a Moment*, the Czech issue of *Modern Poetry in Translation*. Primarily known as a poet, she has also published a collection of short stories and written a several theatre plays.

Her poetry debut *Ludwig* (1999) and her second collection *Není nutné, abyste mě navštěvoval* (There Is No Need for You to Visit Me, 2001) established her as one of the most distinctive voices in contemporary Czech poetry and introduced her preoccupations and recurrent themes, and the hallmarks of her style: direct, sensual, erotic, but also self-ironic and playful. Her work, whether poetry, prose or drama, mostly speaks from a female perspective, yet referencing quintessentially male influences such as Thomas Bernhard or Ernst Jandl, with an acceptance of the fundamental aloneness and absurdity of human existence, but also with an acknowledgement of the absurd as a dadaist and surrealist legacy.

*Ludwig* was inspired by Berhard's play *Ritter-Dene-Voss* about two sisters awaiting the arrival of their brother, the eponymous Ludwig, who is returning from a mental institution in Vienna. The play, which alludes to the Wittgenstein family, was written for the three actors who appeared in its first staging in 1986 and whose surnames gave the play its title. The play, practically unknown in English-speaking countries, was staged in Prague in the 1990s by J. A. Pitínský, a playwright, dramaturg and director known for his versions of Kafka's work and his unconventional direction of classics. Rudčenková remembers how she became obsessed with the play and was compelled to see it over and over again, fascinated by Bernhard's writing, his 'stubborn pessimism, his depiction of pathological relationships, his angry nihilism, the way he wrote about the dark side of Austria, the dark side of life itself'.

At the same time, she cites the iconic Czech poets, Vladimír Holan and Jiří Orten, as her influences, along with Zbyněk Hejda and Viola Fischerová, who were both included in the *Six Czech Poets* anthology. While Holan and Orten, a generation apart, started writing in the 1930s, Hejda and Fischerová, both of whom could be described as living in exile, one banned from publishing, the other an émigré, were unable to reach a wider readership until after the regime change of 1989, and influenced the young generation of poets coming of age in the 'post-Velvet' era. With their inclination towards dark pessimism on the one hand and surrealism on the other, these influences are evident in Rudčenková work, as is inspiration by folklore. Where she writes about fear of old age, her words resonate with Fischerová's poems about the decline of the female body, while her surreal, dreamlike visions are reminiscent of Hejda's work, and the tragic lyricism of some of the poems are a tribute to Orten, with whom she openly identifies: 'I was Orten, and I died under the wheels of cars', referring to the untimely death of the poet at the age of twenty-two. Another source of equally tragic inspiration, in her own words, was Ivan Blatný who lived and died in England where he spent much of his time in hospitals and mental institutions, and whose selected poems were posthumously published in English translation in 2007.

In her third collection *Popel a slast* (Ashes and Pleasure, 2004), which includes the poem 'Dream of a journey' that gave the name to this selection, her vision oscillates between stylised, almost voyeuristic eroticism and existential reflection on the short-lived nature of erotic passion that always leads to a state of aloneness and necessitates emotional self-sufficiency. The title poem ushers in a theme of reconciliation with the ephemeral nature of existence and the motif of walking through a landscape which is developed almost into a ritual in her last collection: 'Peace is in the dying / that shrouds us. Mist / over woods, slow conversation / slow walking, us.'

In the same year, she published her short story collection *Noci, noci* (Nights, Nights) which, like her poetry and plays, speaks of a young woman's desires and the tensions, frustrations and disappointments inherent in relationships, while it foregrounds a sensibility rooted in emotional traumas of childhood and youth, as in the story 'Forest', included in the anthology of Czech woman's short fiction in English translation, *Povídky*: 'Destructive dreams about Mother, erotic dreams about Father ... In my dream I saw Mother devoured by flames. Lying on a grassy hill, she kept sinking through the earth.'

When asked about working with different genres, the author admits that she has been writing exclusively plays for some time and that she may not be returning to poetry in the foreseeable future. In her dramatic texts, as in her poetry and prose, she has been preoccupied with social and cultural constructs of female identity and the elusive fulfilment male-female relationships promise but never deliver. Her first play *Frau in Blau* (2004), for example, examines Alma Mahler's relationship with artist Oskar Kokoschka and focuses on Mahler's unborn daughter. The theme of childlessness appears also in her poetry: 'In the metal-frame bed of lovers that will never produce any young / inhibited by the ghosts of their parents' separate beds', where the principles of passion and pleasure are at odds with the constraints marriage and motherhood impose on women.

The three protagonists of the play *Čas třešňového dýmu* (The Time of the Cherry Smoke, 2007), the result of a residency at the Royal Court Theatre in London, are a daughter, mother and grandmother, brought together to resolve their differences. They are mirrored in three classic fairy-tale characters – Cinderella, Snow White and Sleeping Beauty – who, echoing *Waiting for Godot*, represent the quintessential bride waiting in vain for the arrival of the bridegroom, already experiencing the disappointment inherent in every wedding that carries in it the seed of future failure.

In her 2007 'play in a play' *Niekur* ('Nowhere' in Lithuanian) the main characters Agnes, a Czech woman writer, and Kornelijus, an older Lithuanian poet, meet at a writers' residency in Germany, where Agnes came to work on what appears to be an absurdist drama featuring conjoined twins, played by the same two actors. References to the Central and Eastern European world of arts and literature, to residencies, reading tours and festivals, make a frequent appearance in her work and are quite openly autobiographical, grounding the text in the specificity of a place and giving rise to speculation about the thinly disguised identity of the male characters. And so it is likely – but also somewhat irrelevant – that the poem 'We drink ashes together' was inspired by the same chapter in the poet's life, which she closes with the words: '... and when you return to your Lithuania in May, you will already be dead to me'.

Her fourth and so far last collection, *Chůze po dunách* (Walking on Dunes, 2013), came almost a decade after her third, winning her the prestigious Magnesia Litera Award and critical praise: 'The imagery with which Rudčenková escapes the prose of everyday life, has the power of a magic formula. Her word is full of colours, it comes alive in the excited flesh, restlessly spills like the sea. Among returns to the roots, to the material of her own childhood, and fleeting anticipations of what could happen in the future, the presence pulsates – insecure, temporary, mortal, yet, the only one that is up for grabs. A mix of romanticism, existentialism, absurd drama. Simply great poetry.'

The dunes of the title reflect the location where part of the collection was written, the coastal town of Ventspils in Latvia she visited on two occasions as resident in the International Writers' and Translators' House. Here the act of walking becomes almost a ritual that calms and allows reflection, ushering in a less exulted, more reconciled tone. But walking and movement are also the key themes carried over from her previous work: always trying to reach the point hidden beyond the horizon, literally avoiding 'stasis' and the restrictions of a stagnant life in favour of existence determined perhaps by uncertainty but also by responsibility towards nothing else than the imperative of inner authenticity.

Alexandra Büchler

FROM

# Ludwig

(1998)

# I know where

I know what makes leaves tremble
I know where fear comes from and sobs
I know that quiet place among the trees

There, where even the bird darting in the sky
feels most abandoned
there, where the water is turbid even on the brightest day

that's where I live. Animal and mute
animated by a desire for anything
since I am all that's empty

since I am pain
a wound full of blood
from which drinks
the day that's not to come

# Sins

There is an area in the world
where everything is dying
that is where he walks,
and there is another where he waits writhing
that is where I walk, alone.

There must be somewhere in the dark
an area of broken glass
glinting darkly into the silence
where what longs to tightly embrace
leans close to find its place.

There, where it is dark,
where you only feel your way
and also perhaps whisper
there walk together those
who until recently were forbidden
to each other.

There, where it is dark,
where you can only feel your way
There, behind the curtain,
terrible, abysmal sins
hold sway.

# Ludwig

Everything reeks of smoke.

A man grown through with
flesh and facial hair and words and glory and illusions.

Like smoke condensed in tree trunks
rising into the branches.

Ludwig is missing here
in the yard, darkness leans against the door
the windows shatter
and from the stone walls of the quarry
sound the wheeze and rattle
of approaching old age.

# It seems

It seems to me that buildings are getting whiter
or greyer
that it's all the more difficult to find someone
just to be silent with
and that it's late

Naked violinists' hesitant strings
sound at the touch of tattered bows
still the same words over and over
the same melodies
wherever you go

# To close one's eyes

First, we had to wait a long time
before relief came, whatever it was
whether prohibition or spleen,
awakened desire or death

We had to think of what had not been,
be in our dreams with those who disappeared

We had to sit for a long time
thinking of the mirrors above
and what reflections they cast

We had to be silent,
we had to speak when there was nothing to say
close our eyes when we most wanted to stare

at trees on the hillside, at flies' nests,
coiled excrement and hissing snakes

when we most wanted to speak.

# Where we slept yesterday

Where we slept yesterday
we lie down again today

Smoke a quality cigar
before falling asleep

fill the room with smoke
don't see each other don't exchange a word

allow ourselves to dream of another place
with another cigar and another body

# As if next to myself...

I want nothing anymore
I expect nothing

Where I was once excited
I now sob
swallowing back tears

An empty person is sad
an indifferent one even sadder

As if something were rotting next to me
As if I lived somewhere next to myself

# Ludwig, a hundredth time

These openings grow deeper
and they hurt.

Will we see each other again
between what door frames
darting through what plot

But the fruit is rotten inside
in fragile shells
crumbles
at the lightest touch
that threadbare trick:

Turn around a hundredth time and leave
responding to the same line
he – branches stripped of leaves
I – leaves reticent towards his drooping
swaying nudity.

# The song death sings to Ludwig

Whether you come quietly
whether you come at all
I want you to fly in flocks
in dense clouds
shrouded in overhanging avalanches

If you come
I want you to flow
unwittingly like a length of hair
from the edge of a bed

If you come darkened in a whale's throat
I want you to appear suddenly
in stark light
like veins bulging on arms

I want to hide
in the shameless embrace
of your shuddering
disintegrating
muscles

# There Is No Need for You to Visit Me

## (2001)

\*\*\*

I'd give anything for Akhmatova to step down
from Petrov-Vodkin's picture, and, continuing to
fix me with that gaze ... lie down by my side
in the dark.

In spring I am visited only by desires.
Nothing left to do but lose myself in things.

*'In spring, all the birds*
*return to Bibirevo.'*

*'Remember how I showed you the man*
*sitting at the head of the table in the Belvedere?'*

The enchantment of direct speech.

# Nowhere

Purple leaves growing all over me
I'll leave my roots underwater.

You'll open the windows, and from a distance
hear the mallet blows, like when
they killed carp here by the vats in winter.

You'll immerse yourself in reading, pondering things
so as not to think about yourself.

You'll feel good inside the voices,
with two sentences left,
the first made from my rib,
the second from yours.

# Nights

Mostly warm nights with windows open wide
are filled with cries and sobs.

Visitors are invisible through treetops.
This is where the year draws to an end.

A student who is a pedestrian in the street
and a drowning man at sea
becomes a tiny saint
in some family alcove.

There, the night has come. You'll know me
by my footsteps and the shape of my shadow.

\*\*\*

I look forward to sleep
as if it let us back out
of life

Evening is reserved for women
A tight, stifling embrace

Bear it a little longer, they promise
as if there were something to wait for

# Early evening

Wedged in each other with the darkest
corners of our bodies
so as to forget.
And punished again by the gluttonous motion
of a torment wildly staring from within.

Each blood contraction is too little.
None of the moans do justice
or capture the voracity.

It keeps coming back
like the voice of the tower clock
so regular
so fierce.

# Early evening II

Everything with which you bend over me
is a victim of evening fires
Be kind,
embrace me in the burning light

\*\*\*

We experienced much in our imagination
The stream swelled and swept the nymphs from its shores
The last ferryman was dragged to the bottom of the maelstrom

The hum of voices and conversations echoes from the underground
A new game is being played

Poetry like a pack of words
unable to resist exposing itself
slipped its white hand under the neckline

\*\*\*

Her again asleep on the wardrobe
in a room flooded with blindness

Groping
while you are being violated by the sun

Thrice it sounds Thrice
ever more pleadingly

Like the way is shown to the blind

# Still tomorrow

Covered pistons, currents, folding screen,
safely hidden we speak from the back.

Desire to touch behind the folding screen,
desire for blood at the table
angular elbow, trident
stone. His head.

To approach again, to be greeted
with a heroic morning gesture.

To be his language, his conscience,
his word.

\*\*\*

Autumn butterfly
plays with a wind chime
in the chrysanthemums.

In a dream dreamt by death
it is we who see ourselves

# Tower

We go up the staircase,
all day long, for many years.
small windows in all four directions,
the northern one facing the sea.

I always climbed faster,
then caught up with you,
then even passed you.
Alone among winding walls
I keep turning back
in case you catch up with me.

# A visit to the sanatorium

Gertude takes me aside
entrusting me with manuscripts rescued from the fire.

An ancistrus dances on the wall
alongside her shadow, as she begs me
– tell him that my name is not Bertha!

Shaking off dust insects from her shoulders
– Bertha … does he ever talk to you
without raving?

A gaping window, a terrace
full of pigeons, animal vortex, then
nothing but Gertrude's charged silence,
the terrace sinks, the room goes up in flames.

# Lunnyi svet

Heads like anglepoise lamps
A face the same colour in the background
A luminescent forest
In that forest a white-walled
    cemetery
Covered with noon shadows
None of which reaches
    as far as the church
And windows, evening-like windows

All that in a single
    turn of the head
Anglepoise, anglepoise
What does it feel like
to be devoured
    in the jaws of a beast?

# Edge

With the movement of the tide, I don't know where
the sea ends and the shore begins,
where another body edges onto mine.

I let torn clothes
hang on me, bread
go mouldy on the bed,
hair grow through a shrub.

We live in an old house
on the edge of nothing in particular,
we live far away in mocking
silence.

# What more

I will name my sheep, my fish,
inner passion disappears because I don't hope.

In my dream I know already which way they go.
They bore me. These reactions, that skansen
in my head. What more can be said?

I wake up in the morning,
The legs of the piano have been cut.
Whatever I name, disappears.

\*\*\*

A woman on the train, talking
to her only son as if to a lover.

Elbows touching. A brief sigh.

'Don't eat it all. We'll travel in the dark.'

# Cabinet

I'm the centre of the room
in which bones are sifted.

The tongues of plants, a silver cupboard.

I lie looking into darkness,
head under the pillow,
an alert animal
that starts relationships by day.

It seems that without us the city doesn't exist.

I belong to no one.
My face is pliable,
a night is enough for me to forget anything.

# Cabinet II

Notebooks of memory and white geography.
And newspapers. And dictionaries,
several journals.

Then I slip under the pillow
next to a handkerchief
and pyjama bottoms
I bury my head.

I am an animal resisting words.

# Borderline shadow

Don't disturb me, I'm asleep.
All that's dead belongs to me.
The sleeper's hand mysteriously limp,
again that fallen hair.

Is this the right country? It smells
of soap, ashes, it's so familiar!
What will I be without words
but a rounded stone.

Every day a cracked step,
reproaches, guilt
entreaties, pleading

a cavity for head
the sound of a funeral bell
a seeming.

# I'll fall asleep

Beyond, there is nothing.
Just sleep, pale twilight
on one's sleeves.

Illicit pallor,
terror of empty walls.
The shadow breaks in a familiar way
where the ceiling starts.

I'll go further, I will, I'll pounce.

Sleep is seaweed,
that slowly suffocates me.
So. Gently. The path ahead
opens like a crater.

\*\*\*

Yes, I live inside the piano.
but there is no need
for you to visit me.

FROM

# Ashes and Pleasure

(2004)

# Ruins

It started with schizophrenia.
The oblique light would daily wake them up.
The house shook with the trams booming past.
Since childhood.

We make ourselves at home, hour after hour.
Here in this heap I lived with my brother.
This is where noise would wake us.
A Christmas tree stood here
and grandmother lived in the kitchen next door.
Steps echoed,
clinking cutlery, running water, laughter,
A comb placed in front of the mirror.
You used to have long hair.

That you would one day pull out books from the ruins, photos,
letters and jewellery.
That you would find there your baby hands, your head,
your sleep and fear.

What we cling to.
As always, destruction.
What we return to.
Walls.

Dust will no longer harm,
don't wipe it away.

# Pendulum

My passions are being covered with lichen,
waves, all these waning waves
but time is not to blame.

And yet again from the deep
a burning light is brought to the surface
I eagerly draw in
its cherry smoke.

Between the bodies of winters
a gap narrows frantically.

I lie on mattresses
like in a wooden coffin.

Within the space of skin, desires,
thoughts, muscles
you no longer see me as a being
but as eternity.

# The image of a copulating couple stayed with you

A woman undressing in the lobby
weary eyes following her from armchairs.
Black suspenders stretch into the night
and snap.

A man is taking her by the mirror
her gaze briefly meets yours.

Frost-covered fields in the early morning.
Round lights in the dining car
are all the moons
you lost thinking of women
that are by now most likely dead.

Outside the windows,
above the mounds of manure,
black birds like widows.
Avenues of trees
leading mercilessly ahead.

# Periphery

The snow slowly vanishes,
it's harder and harder not to ask you.
Or rather – not to admit
that I never stare into the distance
except when it's impossible.

And so, the land where I hide
is not alive,
I drag behind me several
endlessly merging scenes.

His bitterness, my silence.
Silhouette of a mountain and bright sunset
that never touch.

# Dream of a journey

Far from all homes,
not even in this land,
we wait for departure,
each to a different place.
I'm only pretending direction.

I let the bus leave,
the lover wait,
alone I walk into the fields,
into the burning fields.

# Always us, always others

Something must have remained
of those shared awakenings
the shared nakedness.
Something must have remained
of those webs of notions
of what the future holds.
Yet, nothing comes to mind.
How ruthlessly it fades away.

And you, are you full of ideas, full of hopes?
And you, are you stroking the past
and the future like two
purring cats
with your warm hands?

# An evening of water

The pool is empty for the winter
yet steps lead down inside it
Waiting for water in water's evening
just before evening and day
a man came to lift me from weeping
and despite being physically close
maintained a semblance of absence.

# A man to define

I dance with him, while he has only a faint idea.
He falls asleep on the couch curled around my hips
eyes wide open under closed lids,
breathing in the flesh. Warm skin and time,
I don't know how it will be stuck
between his body and mine,
as he lowers his head through many years
to press his lips against my neck, the time and weight
of that last month of my loneliness
to pour into me desire and pride
of a lifetime of being alone.

# Out of words

What if he looks
from behind different eyes?
What if time flows
faster in his body
and he has the spine of an old man?

The scalding sea washes him,
he no longer laments, just clings on,
The night is clasped inside him,
he is hammered out of words
and goes on hammering.

# A man to define II

Did you more go out to encounter, or did you wait?
Were you more of a doer, or were you done to?

Is the body sleeping in the grass relying
on us to wake it?

To whom are you writing all this?
Who should hear you, to whom did you give yourself?

My back under his palm,
like warmth taking hours to penetrate
the walls of a frozen house at the end of winter,
when we have finally arrived.

# Between a tree and Pär

We walk through darkness
find the corridor to the underground
in which I sense a spiral staircase without railings
and shreds of skin.
It's dawn and the arch
of open sky is torn.

You tell me the story of how as children
you and your two years younger brother
secretly slipped into the workshop of your carpenter father,
and your brother accidentally cut off your little finger
with one of his metal tools.
My brother once nearly strangled me.

Both stories merge in this evening
and our two murderous brothers suddenly meet on the meadow
with lanterns in their hands and a sweet inkling
that their siblings
are taking a walk together on a clearing in eternity.

# The birch tree and water

Breathless, surrounded by walls,
the way you will be in the future together
again.

Darkness has plunged in the water with you,
pressing its cold breasts to your lips,
her hair bristles, your sombre excitement
makes her gasp.

Together not only where she can
no longer force her way between your
skin on skin.

How she could slowly stroke your
sex with the sole of her foot
making it harden like the glass in windows
on which the wind taps.

Why don't you wish for anything?
You have locked yourselves in here, and the laughter of those
who envy your dark intimacy leans heavily against the door.
You are drunk.

As soon as the bark of your dress
reveals a white shoulder,
the black stiletto has slipped off your foot
the heel pointing towards the ceiling, the sky.
The foot has already plunged,
instead of it and instead of the darkness
the death from your dream came
to lie down with you in the hot water,
a desirable woman in white
who took you away holding your hand
exactly as you had wished.

# Of time

As a child I had life in front of me
without knowing it.
By the sea I learnt to plunge headlong
into the water from the rocks.

A year then lasted forever.

Today, only unbearable
moments last forever.

My grandmother's longest year
was in the second grade.

At your age, said grandmother,
I didn't think about the passage of time at all.
I only do now.

I do think about it, granny. It's faster and faster.
I am also not getting any younger,
I can see it on my skin, in my hair
and yet I am still far from that proper life
everybody has expected me to live since childhood.

Just don't force anything, said grandmother
and headed for the kitchen to pour us some more wine
which – as we chat –
imperceptibly ferments.

\*\*\*

I celebrated life on the shore
in a surf of excitement and sun
my body scrubbed
free of old bitterness

As my dreams leaned on stones
flowed down my slender fingers
in white spume

The sea rose like fireworks
between my thighs
clusters of sea snails clinging to a rock
sat tightly beside me

I wasn't alone in the waves
future time moved the cove
the smooth weave of water
knew of my blood.

# Island

Three times we walked around the island
and we are still walking.
The fishermen are returning,
dusk falls into the boats.
They hang the dead mackerel back on the hooks
and photograph themselves with their catch on the shore.

We still don't know which
is the one with a wooden leg.
The drunk one, who fell asleep on the pier?

# Grape and storm

The dog's barking
sharply stabs at the lonely figure
in the middle of the vineyard.
Lightning strikes, without rain or thunder.
Something is about to happen,
but it never does.

The glowing lamps along the road
become blurred lines of lights
under eyelashes.

The sound of cicadas returns me to the island
where in the night I dreamt about a different life.

Here in Medana I am part of the sky,
my consciousness burns bright then vanishes
with the headlights of the oncoming cars.

# Animals

I've always found your greedy eyes frightening
My longing for peace
cannot be simply surrounded with conifer branches

Nothing happens
apart from exaggerated gestures

Everywhere someone sitting and talking on the phone
announcing a great mood and immortality

\*\*\*

I never stay with
whoever accompanies me

I kill the mosquitoes on the walls
draw the curtain
touch the room and objects borrowed from life
with my eyes

The sea is as far away as the hope
that I will return to its shores

# Come nightfall

That evening stream of people with their lingering voices
the diminishing light withdrawing from the streets
I don't want to grow old like the woman at the next table
whose lines are as deep as the pattern of her partner's pullover
I don't want to grow old like the woman at the second table
whose hair resembles a wig
more than a wig could ever resemble hair
I don't want my face to be lost in the shop window of spectacles
and most of all I don't want the feeling of my own body
tight like an uncomfortable sea cabin
all those radiant people and wrecks I among them
exposing my body to the sun
and my life to random explanations.

# Natural processes

Since I have not been going out,
the journey from my room to the bathroom
has become a thrilling adventure.

# Shroud, birch tree, white dress

You who at night peel off
paint from cracked walls
When you were still beautiful
and untouched
you already felt that your belly was full of ashes

Things since then have moved away from you
to the extent that they no longer remind you of anything

There is still hope
but you walk around it lightly
as if around a lake
where you sense
a smiling drowned woman
lying in the reeds

\*\*\*

To remind me that it is possible
to find enthusiasm and excitement
even here in Europe, even without men, without art,
a nun spoke to me in a dream
about ordinary things
with childlike zeal.

# Movement, hardness

You haven't witnessed
frantic changes lately
just minor shifts.

We walk.

The round stone
we found during our stroll through the woods
may hide a gem.

But that's no reason to break it.

# All poems end in death

Don't touch the door through which he enters,
he's only come to make up for the nights
that found you writhing with desire
and press down on your spine.
Are you now unable to adopt the form
in which he at the same time disappears? Be calm.
Think of the space
where the courtyard touches the buildings,
look around you, sometimes you dream
about his body's death.

I'll never write my way out of my yearning
which turns into a vicious bedraggled cat
with a blood-stained mouth. Probably a bird or a moth.

# The lover and eyes

His fingerprints remained on the glass table surface,
ashes of burned cherry tobacco on the windowsill,
the disturbed texture of dust where he had moved.
The memory of pleasure fades first.
His footprints in the snow in which I walked,
once more passing the fence with a torn glove.
Drastic, I tell myself, just so drastic,
caught in a trap,
dirty and alone.
It could have also been a bird
with blood-stained feathers
if nature were in the mood
for signs.

# Will and subconscious

You scream in terror in your dream,
because an unknown female figure is moving your bed, your whole body.

What's so frightening about it, you say in daylight,
she wasn't a monster or a freak.

As if you didn't understand that alien control
of your body
is the beginning of clear lunacy.

# We drink ashes together

We sit among Germans,
and, so that they don't understand us,
because we don't understand them,
you, a Lithuanian, speak Polish
and I reply in Czech.

Last night you watched a film with Lara Croft
she was pretty, you say,
towards the end, the story moved to Siberia
Lara ran around on graves
wearing just a T-shirt with short sleeves.

Siberia is your birthplace, you were the first-born,
Siberia is where your father slept with his hair in snow drifts,
Siberia is where your mother grew up,
that's where they met.
Your brother, a sculptor, made his imprint in stone.

You are now forty-four and your grey hair
is soft like moss and ash
that falls soundlessly into a kettle
placed on the floor,
when you smoke by the window at night
and the wind doesn't want to take it.

I'm not saying that I am preparing to die today
But why has the idea that one day we will each die
in our own country crossed my mind so many times?
Who will dance naked on our graves?

When we reach the lake, it's March,
sun and bracing wind,
you take off your clothes.
Your firm body gleams on the shore,
you run into the freezing water.
When you return to your Lithuania in May
you will already be dead to me.

# Ashes and pleasure

Peace is in the dying
that shrouds us. Mist
over woods, slow conversation,
slow walking, us.

Nights together,
when you listen to the breathing
and watch the face sunk
in the thoughts of a floating brain.
Everything open consoles us:
fields, sky, the surface of lakes and seas.

Sinking in you. Pleasure, lightning.
Rising on knees and hands.

You can no longer tell
a sigh of pleasure from a whine,
rhythmical steps following a coffin
from the thrusts of love.

# Ice, heat, a funeral in each movement

Today the birds have unlearned how to fly
they walk on the ground
the barking of a dog on the edge of the village is heartrending

Only you know, God, whether we shall move
and if it were indeed us
I don't pay attention to signs

No more narrow beds
No more hard ground

The rhythmical ride of bodies
we were fine in the underworld
you must not turn around, search for her secret
you won't be ferried across twice
even if your singing melts the rocks.

# Daylight encounter

She emerged from the far end of the wood.
She watched her approach across the mounds of grass
as in the past. Minuscule tremors,
reminiscent of nothing,
nothing at all.

'I had a dream', she said
'in which we had a son together.
You were full of reproach
as if against a father neglecting his child.
You were your own mother, I your father'.

She laid her down on the grass
and placed her palm on her belly.
She pressed her head against it
and from that position,
feeling her relaxed breathing,
watched the golden wheat
sway in the breeze.

# The miracle of dual movement

We with tragic eyes
are capable of disappearing in what is seen.
For example, glancing at stones around a lake
we become stones around a lake.
But what are then returns to consciousness?

When you plunge below the surface,
at the same time you soar into the sky
in its still reflection.

# Burying pleasure

A body with ribcage
void of viscera pretends to be intact
beneath the suit.
And that is human beauty.

Physical memory
vanishes fastest.

Tables invisibly collapsing
under our dishes.
The gravedigger does his work unwittingly,
decay and his glance
full of unconscious pleasure.

# Spring and death

Each blooming shrub means that the hair turns a denser grey
the newly dead leaving on boats
for magical villages above the canals.

Journeys should also soothe you,
making you lose a sense of your disintegration
in the multicoloured world.
What you emanate
returns to you,
and so, children gather around you in spring,
adults in summer
and in autumn, a tight gaggle of old men presses you
against a door behind which music can be heard,
memories seem like firm ropes of
your consciousness,
yet
they are mere reflections of the winter sun
on the fragmented surface of water.

# Sadness

Fountains singing in cities,
far away from us.
Their music, which we dream about,
is magnificent.

The forest – all space and regularity.

Deep fountains, black wells with grills on top
echo the wind that passes them by,
dragging its whistling voice over their rims.

We pass the forest, gently leaning forward as we ride.

The singing will reach this village across the flat fields.

What should I think about this spring
that arouses nothing in me.
Probably the same I think about this avenue of trees,
about multicoloured parrots in cages,
all untouched by my absence.

# In sounds, in the face

Every afternoon he goes to play the grand piano in the museum
I see him through the window,
a swirl of fine down,
at other times I watch him from inside,
as he reads newspapers in the castle park.

We who are not in a battle with the times,
but with ourselves,
are only dangerous to ourselves.

Gusty wind, bells, the end of everything.
I hide from sadness in the garden,
it reaches me with sound.

I will set out from here on a long journey on foot,
by sea, sleeping anywhere in the grass.
When dirt and fatigue have smoothed my face,
I'll come home pure and become something.

# Burying pleasure, the real face

I am still going, yes,
but with my body half sunk underground,
so my lap is always covered with cool soil.

The heat of my hips is voracious,
my real face
is damp shade, semidarkness, the heavy smell of mould and smoke.

# Disintegration of time

Suddenly, it was not possible
to keep consciousness composed.
The bed on which they slept
under a white blanket
hiding evidence of orgasms.
At night they danced, by day they slept.
Then they left.
It was no longer possible to prove it.

# The dying of the day

It's over.
A step towards passion frozen in Easter fire.
Statues, free of their wooden winter attire
have nothing more to remove. Like us.
Whatever didn't happen, wasn't possible.

# The dying of the day II

Why do they come out of the house,
when they don't feel the need to move?
Why do they converse without the need to speak?

Sometimes they listen to distant music,
seeping through closed doors and windows,
merging with the cockerel's crowing.
The reasons at best accidental.
No, they didn't expect anything. Not at the start.

Why do they look around when they don't expect anything new?
Why do they die when living was not their choice?

FROM

# Walking on Dunes

(2013)

\*\*\*

My apartment is floating away
with paddles of light stripes
cast by cars passing in the street below,
it's floating away like a darkroom
with its beakers of chemicals,
I see it clearly, full of suffocating water.
In the metal-frame bed of lovers that will never produce any young,
inhibited by the ghosts of their parents' separate beds.
The apartment is floating, carrying me in its nothingness,
in which a snail drags with it the inseparable history of shells.
I was Orten and I died under the wheels of cars,
now I am the silhouette of strange flowers
I grew from seed.

\*\*\*

These parents
who are these strangers
who have descended into apartment nests
where their children lived long before
these parents, flapping birds
where did they come from
they have colourful feathers
nobody recognises them,
their talk is harsh cackling
and they feign familiality.

# Missing the orange carpet she grew up on

longing for a centre, for the jubilant yellow yolk,
for which she has aimed since the egg-whites of birth

during the day fitting into a mould like orderly
    confectionery
at night being blown in bubbles up to the indecent
    sky
to float, light as a feather
bathe in the candyfloss maker
in tablets of vice

to love fairground dodgems
the safety of a little car that's never going to arrive

\*\*\*

Childhood and its dreams
soda bottles in crates at the mountain chalet
cold pantry smell full of hopes
new words and new ideas...

But the zenith you are aiming for
has long since gone,
they tell you a few years later.

And you, quite naturally,
go on
waiting...

Frozen snow on a roof
just before it slides down.

# The imperceptible fading away

The substance of time, avalanche of black snow
we are caught in:
red rosehips among black boughs,
belugas under ice.

The imperceptible fading away
as you fall asleep and wake up,
the fading passion,
and growing demand for trust

and in the corner that swelling yearning
for an even more fundamental meaning of life,
for an even more noble self-fulfilment,
with less and less ability and interest
to achieve it all.

\*\*\*

In a dream I look down
at the wide Chinese river at dawn,
intoxicatingly bright lanterns swaying above it.
I have to write a poem about this right now, I tell myself,
before I wake up,
before the first light –
while it's all still true.

# The necessity of carnival

*for Ivanka and Erik*

The night erupted in wildness, like every carnival night. Sensuous tongues sprouted out of walls, tables began to move of their own volition. Some people fell asleep in the early evening only to wake up at night with fiery masks on their faces. They walk along scaffolding and bar counters, voluntary sleepwalkers, they saddle up a deer, and break their bones without any fuss in the name of a higher cause, they want to reach higher, free themselves, give thanks for the life rising inside their bodies, make visible the greatness only they know about, shout it all out... They undress and get dressed again as the other sex that opens up in their groins. Men cry and kiss each other, women give themselves roughly. They allow a patch of bare skin to be briefly caressed by those whom they avoid (by day) like their own conscience. Their shadow life, that parallel curriculum vitae of their persistent imaginings, comes alive again, makes somersaults, rules, roars, burns in glasses of boiling wine, reaches up in suppressed energy, strokes the fluorescent strip of light on the ceiling with its fingertips, and, for a brief moment, they achieve their aim: their opposite essence. With bright eyes, softened features, dancing hands like velvet flowers, they argue aggressively about ways of life, at first defending their own to their last breath, out of fear they criticise the lived reality of others, and then they joyfully dismiss their own. All this is done with gusto, so that they can return tomorrow cleansed, each to a different place, their cave of hidden thoughts swept clean, because they already know what would happen if they followed them, their broken bones set, blood dried, relieved to have escaped much greater misfortune, presumed sin, with the humility of ashes that secretly respect the power of their all-destroying fire and so cultivate it consciously at carnival time.

# Other people's aquariums

What I like about other people's apartments is that the way
    objects are arranged in space is given, I can only
    watch them be.
What makes me nervous in my own apartment is the opposite –
    nothing is definitive.
As in life. The fragility, the vulnerability of the way things are
    today.
I could, theoretically, move anything
at any time. My things, clothes, wardrobes and tables
    are suffused with the provisional nature of my existence
    here on earth, with my uncertainty, my mortality.
I uncritically accept all aquariums belonging to other people
    (as long as there is no plastic castle inside)
    only I cannot come to terms with my own aquarium, it appears
    dark, its dirt falls on my head,
I witness dying fish that I then
    have to throw down the toilet,
the flowers in it have to be endlessly moved around,
    replaced with new ones because they turn yellow.
Yet, I keep it alive for years, buy
    new fish, keep them warm, clean the sand and stones
    unable to stop. Of course, until it cracks
    and the water pours out I will never voluntarily
    liquidate my aquarium.

# Private carnival

Some men enter strange women's apartments, immediately
    taking off their clothes at the entrance, and, in the semi-darkness
    of rooms with ancestors' portraits and historical
    furniture, display their nudity.
The women gaze at them intently like voyeurs
    with bated breath,
as the solemn-faced men in front of them
    pull at their sex with that familiar sliding movement,
and, despite their dignified posture
    resemble perverts in parks, Spanish
    exhibitionists in narrow side streets
    away from the tourist beaten track,
    who satisfy themselves quickly as they walk in the opposite direction...
But these men do not attack, they are free of violence, they simply wish to be
    viewed with kindness by the desiring women. This seems to be
    more intimate than the sex act itself.
They have just briefly left their families and children, at home
    no one has looked at them for a long time.
The women live forever in a tower,
they welcome such a spectacle any time,
waiting for an orgasm they nonchalantly take
    for granted,
free of lust, they are patiently curious and they themselves
    have beautiful but tired eyes.

# The unseen fireworks

You didn't go out.
Everything was too easily imagined
in advance.

All you heard was a booming sound: the fireworks
splashed across the sky outside your field of vision.

You watched the square, people
running in the night to catch the celebration.

Fascinated by the trust
which propelled them towards that happiness of light
in an unequivocally black sky.

\*\*\*

In a fisherman's house
you felt a stranger's vanished life in your pores,
you were lying down quietly like smooth wood
on the floor your body full of rings and knots,
witness to the ancient growth and expansion of branches.

Your memory in the memory of the barn
smelling of slaughter
of animal carcasses
that fed
the living,
who died only a few years after their cattle.

\*\*\*

Perhaps you yourself are the red light of the lighthouse
that doesn't let ships and planes collide
and you don't even know it.

Perhaps it's you who guards the land.

Perhaps it's at your foot
that seagull eggs
are laid for an intimate dinner.

It's possible that in your grass
on the dunes – in that one place in the world –
flocks of rare birds have their nests.

Step back.
Your solitude at the tip of the South Pier
has a deeper meaning
than mere loneliness.

# Ventspils, the end of the word

I reached the end of the world, where the path ends,
or if it doesn't, it's the same.

Between the pine forest sprouting from the dunes
and the sea commanding the land, nagging it
then taking back its request,
the sea, which alone in itself
in its capricious movement
carries eternity,
amidst dry trunks and stones
the endlessly nodding grass
a rope stood out, stretched there from the old days
of vanished fishing villages.

Seagulls hung there in the air without moving
    from the spot
waving their wings with great effort against the airstream.

The mass of water gleaming again,
on the horizon a boat inched forward at a snail's pace,
never to reach its destination, that was
    certain,
or maybe in a few years, it seemed, given its speed.

Three years of trusting closeness,
a piece of the reef broken off
leaving no trace in water or on land.
Except bitterness carried by the wind
sticking to the palate, except a few grey leaves of grass
in the sand's hair,
except surprised seagulls steadying themselves
high up above this sudden chasm of empty
    space.

So much effort and yet remaining in the same spot,
the same intensity requiring
more and more energy and time.

The snail ship finally disappeared from the horizon.
And the journey back – walking the shoreline for hours,
retracing my footprints, testifying to my decision
to always reach the
    most remote
visible point.

# Walking on dunes

Even though you were moved
by the intense shade of green
of the trees and grass and pine-tree undergrowth

even though you were moved by this summer's nostalgia of smoke
burning grass and baked fish

even though you were moved by the children
who, still innocent of the restrictions of the world,
were already skipping
from one tile of the same colour to another,

yet underneath all that emotion
you remained cold in your disappointment
like an icy pool in a Siberian forest.

You kept turning to make sure
that the footprints left in the sand had been washed away,
washed away, you weren't. You didn't want to be,
you didn't want to leave your imprint in anything at all.

# Amber heads

Looking in vain for amber among seaweed
on Ventspils shore
ended with success in a dream:
in the desert, on the plain, among little figurines
sold by the locals on their stalls, she discovered
translucent candle holders, chiselled faces, entire heads
made of huge pieces of amber.
Radiating a suffused, intoxicating golden glow
arousing a feeling of sheer fulfilment: happiness.

# Boat

As the ant dragged the dried-out husk of a dead beetle
up the sandy slope – hollow, headless
we watched our empty wooden boat
bob up and down on the distant horizon of the sea.

# Notes

**Introduction:** The author's statements are based on email correspondence between the translator and author. The critical quote is from a review of the author's last collection by the Czech critic Radim Kopáč.

**Lunnyi svet:** The title of the poem means 'Moonlight' in Russian and refers to a book featuring paintings, among them the portrait of Anna Akhmatova by Kuzma Petrov-Vodkin. The voice here is of a male subject, which is grammatically signalled in the original Czech, but can't be reproduced in English.

**My apartment is floating away:** This untitled poem makes reference to Jiří Orten (1919-1941), a talented Czech Jewish poet who died tragically at the age of twenty-two as a result of a street accident, having published three collections. A prestigious prize for young authors under thirty was established in 1987 in his name. The author cites him as one of her key influences.

# Acknowledgements

Alexandra Büchler would like to thank Bernie Higgins, Alvin Pang and Jan Zikmund for their valuable feedback on the translations in this selection.

Translations of some of the poems in this selection, previously published in the following anthologies, have been reworked by the translator.

*A Fine Line: New Poetry from Eastern & Central Europe*, Arc Publications, 2004
'I'd give anything for Akhmatova to step down' / 'Nowhere' / 'Nights' / 'A woman on the train' / 'Yes, I live inside the piano' / 'I look forward to sleep' / 'A visit to the sanatorium' / 'Lunnyi svet' (as 'Holy Moon')

*Six Czech Poets*, Arc Publications, 2008
'I'd give anything for Akhmatova to step down' / 'Nights' / 'A visit to the sanatorium' / 'The image of a copulating couple stayed with you' / 'Always us always, the others' / 'Of words' / 'Birch tree and water' / 'Come nightfall' / 'Movement, hardness' / 'All poems end in death' / 'Lover and eyes' / 'Will and subconscious' / 'Ashes and pleasure' / 'Burying pleasure, true face' / 'Daylight encounter' / 'Disintegration of time'

*The World for a Moment: Focus on Czech Poetry*, Modern Poetry in Translation, No 2, 2020
'Walking on dunes' / 'Perhaps you yourself are the red light of the lighthouse' / 'In a dream I look down' / 'Other people's aquariums'

# PARTHIAN *Poetry in Translation*

## Home on the Move
Two poems go on a journey
Edited by Manuela Perteghella
and Ricarda Vidal
ISBN 978-1-912681-46-4
£8.99 | Paperback
'One of the most inventive and necessary
poetry projects of recent years...'
– **Chris McCabe**

## Pomegranate Garden
A selection of poems by Haydar Ergülen
Edited by Mel Kenne, Saliha Paker
and Caroline Stockford
ISBN 978-1-912681-42-6
£8.99 | Paperback
'A major poet who rises from [his] roots to touch
on what is human at its most stripped-down,
vulnerable and universal...'
– **Michel Cassir**, *L'Harmattan*

## Modern Bengali Poetry
Desire for Fire
Arunava Sinha
ISBN 978-1-912681-22-8
£11.99 | Paperback
This volume celebrates over one hundred years
of poetry from the two Bengals represented
by over fifty different poets.

# PARTHIAN *Poetry*

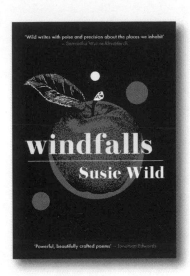

## Windfalls

SUSIE WILD
ISBN 978-1-912681-75-4
£9.00 • Paperback

'Powerful, beautifully crafted poems...
there's nothing like poetry to cut down
the spaces between us, to leap across gaps,
make a friend of a stranger.'
**– Jonathan Edwards**

## Small

NATALIE ANN HOLBOROW
ISBN 978-1-912681-76-1
£9.99 • Paperback

'Shoot for the moon? Holborow has landed,
roamed its face, dipped into the craters, and
gathered an armful of stars
while up there.'
**– Wales Arts Review**